WITHDRAWN

Learning Resources Center
University of Wyoming Libraries
Laramie, WY 82070

HONG KONG

951.25
Lyl

MAJOR WORLD NATIONS
HONG KONG

Garry Lyle

CHELSEA HOUSE PUBLISHERS
Philadelphia

Chelsea House Publishers

Copyright © 1999 by Chelsea House Publishers,
a division of Main Line Book Co.
All rights reserved.
Printed in Hong Kong

First Printing.

1 3 5 7 9 8 6 4 2

Library of Congress Cataloging-in-Publication Data

Lyle, Garry.
Hong Kong / Garry Lyle.
p. cm. — (Major world nations)
Includes index.
Summary: Describes the history, geography, economy, daily life,
and people of the island of Hong Kong.
ISBN 0-7910-4990-6 (hardcover)
1. Hong Kong (China)—Juvenile literature. [1. Hong Kong
(China)] I. Title. II. Series.
DS796.H74L925 1998
951.25—dc21 98-15073
CIP
AC

ACKNOWLEDGEMENTS

The Author and Publishers are grateful to the Hong Kong Tourist Association for
assistance in the preparation of this book and for permission to reproduce copyright
photographs. Other photographs are reproduced by permission of:
Ian A. Griffiths; Geoffrey Howard; Luke McGuinniety and Geoffrey Sherlock.

4

CONTENTS

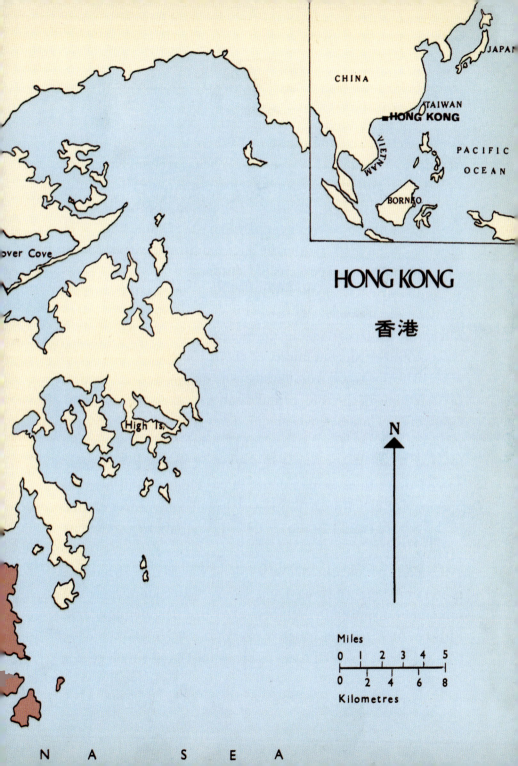

CHINA

JAPAN

TAIWAN
■ HONG KONG

PACIFIC

OCEAN

VIETNAM

BORNEO

over Cove

High Is.

HONG KONG

香港

N

Miles

0   1   2   3   4   5

0   2   4   6   8

Kilometres

N A   S E A

FACTS AT A GLANCE

Land and People

Official Name Hong Kong

Location In the South China Sea, off the southeastern tip of China

Area 945 square miles (2408 square kilometers)

Climate Subtropical

Population 6,491,000

Population Density 15,396.9 per square mile (5,945 per square kilometer)

Mountains Lantan Peak (Fung Wong Shan), Sunset Peak (Tai Tung Shan), Victoria Peak

Official Languages Chinese, English

Ethnic Groups Chinese (97 percent); small numbers of Europeans, Americans, Indians

Religions Predominately Buddhist, Taoist and Confucianist; about a half-million Christians; small number of Muslims and Hindus

Literacy Rate	88 percent
Average Life Expectancy	75.9 years for males; 81.5 years for females

Economy

Natural Resources	Labor force
Division of Labor Force	80 percent service industries; 10 percent manufacturing
Industries	Finance, trade, services, construction, light manufacturing
Major Imports	Machinery, transport equipment, telecommunications equipment, fabric
Major Exports	Textiles, clothing, electrical machinery, office machines, telecommunications equipment
Major Trading Partners	China, Japan, United States, Taiwan, Singapore, Germany, United Kingdom, South Korea
Currency	Hong Kong dollar

Government

Form of Government	Special administrative region of the People's Republic of China
Government Bodies	Legislative Council, currently appointed by selection committee appointed by China
Formal Head of State	Chief executive

HISTORY AT A GLANCE

221 B.C.   Chin Dynasty permanently incorporates Canton area into Chinese Empire.

618-907 A.D.   Under the Tang Dynasty, Canton is connected by roads to major cities to the north. After the fall of the Tang, China breaks up into separate kingdoms and the Canton area is once again isolated.

1283-1288   After establishing themselves as the Yuan Dynasty, the Mongols use the Pearl River area to launch expeditions to Vietnam and Java.

1500s   Japanese pirates raid the Pearl River area.

1557   European traders begin sailing up the Pearl River to Canton. The Portuguese are granted a base on Macao.

1713   British traders become established in Canton, for the time being bypassing Hong Kong.

1800-1809   Vietnamese pirates raid Pearl River area.

1839   The British and Portuguese have been importing Indian opium into China for some time. A new Chinese governor in Canton attempts to end the opium trade by force. After a series of clashes, the British merchants retreat down the Pearl River and anchor at Hong Kong.

1841 Defending British merchants involved in the opium trade, the British are victorious in a series of battles with the Chinese and Hong Kong Island is occupied (January 26).

1842 The Treaty of Nanking opens Shanghai, Canton and other ports to English traders and cedes Hong Kong to Britain "in perpetuity" (as stated in the treaty originally).

1858-1860 A Second Opium War leads to a treaty expanding Western trading rights in China. The Chinese sign the Treaty of Peking, which cedes to the British "in perpetuity" the Kowloon area on the mainland next to Hong Kong Island.

1898 The Chinese cede to the British a mainland area north of Kowloon known as the New Territories. The British only ask for a 99-year lease instead of "in perpetuity," thus laying the groundwork for the eventual return of the colony to China.

1899 Brief period of rioting in the New Territories against British rule. Through another oversight in the leasing agreement, the British have no legal authority over the Walled City area of Kowloon, which remains a center of crime and intrigue until 1976.

1907 British ban opium trade.

1926 Nationalist boycott of Hong Kong.

1927 Fighting breaks out between Chinese Nationalists

and Communists, beginning with Nationalist attacks on Communists in Shanghai.

1941 Japanese forces attack Hong Kong and British forces surrender after two weeks of hard fighting (December 25th).

1945 Japanese occupation forces surrender on August 17, although British forces do not actually arrive until August 30.

1947-1949 A civil war in China between the Communists and Nationalists leads to many people fleeing to Hong Kong, providing a new labor force and expanded market for manufactured products.

1950s Britain uses Hong Kong as a base for operations against Communist forces in Korea and Malaya. An embargo on Chinese goods forces the colony to develop many new industries to be self-reliant.

1962 Relations are strained between China and British authorities, as the Communists attempt to destabilize Hong Kong by encouraging immigration.

1966-1967 The Cultural Revolution in China takes place.

1975 Boat people, refugees from Vietnam, many of Chinese ancestry, begin arriving in the colony in large numbers, creating a strain on social services.

1984 After two years of negotiations, Great Britain and China issue a Joint Declaration regarding the return of Hong Kong to Chinese rule. Hong Kong would become a Special Administrative Region and retain its political and economic system for at least fifty years.

1988 The Chinese government issues a Basic Law regarding the administration of Hong Kong after 1997.

1989 The Chinese government launches a violent crackdown on student protestors in Beijing and reverses some political and economic reforms.

1997 The handover of Hong Kong to China by Great Britain takes place on schedule (June 30).

1998 New modern airport complex opens on small island close to Lantau Island.

1

Only an Island?

If you were asked the question "When is an island not an island?" you could safely answer, "When it is Hong Kong."

The map will help you make sense of that, and it will also show you that there is certainly a Hong Kong Island. It lies in the South China Sea, very near to the coast of China, and about 20 miles (32 kilometers) from the huge mouth of the Pearl River, which leads to the seaport city of Canton.

Canton—or Kwangchow (Guangzhou) to give it its proper Chinese name—was the first Chinese seaport to attract European traders. Early in the nineteenth century, it had a prosperous British community of about 150 people. But in the year 1839 the whole community was driven out of the city, because some of the traders had disobeyed an important command of the Chinese government. They fled down the river in ships, and at last found refuge in the beautiful, sheltered harbor of Hong Kong Island. Later, the Chinese government agreed to let them settle ashore. Hong Kong Island became a colony of the British Empire—a small and nearly empty island colony barely 29 square miles (76 square kilometers) in area.

The Central District of Hong Kong.

To many people, the colony is still only an island. So modern visitors arriving at Hong Kong's busy waterside airport are sometimes surprised to find themselves in a densely-populated little territory, most of which is part of the Asian mainland—a region about fourteen times as big as the island which gave it its name. The region of Hong Kong contains Hong Kong Island, the mainland city of Kowloon, and an area much larger than both, called the New Territories.

There are also no less than 235 other islands in the territory. One, Lantau, is bigger than Hong Kong Island itself, but nearly all the rest are too tiny and barren to be inhabited.

Including all those islands, the total area of Hong Kong is 410 square miles (1,062 square kilometers)—though perhaps it might be safer to say that 410 square miles is the area at present. Because Hong Kong has been reclaiming land from the sea, it is now nearly twelve square miles (31 square kilometers) bigger than it was in 1968, and five square miles (thirteen square kilometers) bigger than it was even in 1978. In the future it should be bigger still. Hong Kong must reclaim land wherever it can, because it is much too small for a population that has grown at an average rate of 125,000 a year since 1945, and is now about six million.

Besides, a great deal of Hong Kong's present land area cannot be used for houses, farms, or factories. Apart from the many pretty but useless little islands, much of the other land is fairly barren, rising very steeply to rocky hills and mountains. Hong Kong Island itself seems to be nearly all mountain, with peaks standing guard at either end. The highest peak, Mount Victoria, overlooks the waterside skyscrapers of the capital city, Central, from a height of 1,809 feet (552 meters). On Lantau Island to the west are Sunset Peak and Lantau Peak (both around 3,000 feet–900 meters) while over on the mainland Tai Mo Shan looks down on them all from 3,144 feet (959 meters).

Tai Mo Shan stands in the northern section of Hong Kong's mainland area, the New Territories. The southern section is very much smaller, and consists mainly of the noisy, overcrowded, industrial city of Kowloon. Kowloon spreads over a wide area of the waterfront opposite Central on Hong Kong Island. It is linked with Central by road and rail tunnels under the vast harbor which lies between. The rail tunnel was opened in 1980, and is part of an underground railway system linking the main parts of the Kowloon area with each other and with Hong Kong Island.

The name Kowloon comes from two Chinese words which mean "nine dragons," but you will not find any dragons in the city– except paper ones at festival times. The nine dragons of the city's name are a range of steep hills which close it in to the north.

Because so much of the land is rocky or steeply hilly, only about 40 square miles (100 square kilometers) of the colony can be used for farming, and some of that is not very fertile. The soil is often short of natural plant-food, and in places lies less than a finger's depth over a bed of solid rock. Even so, the farmland of the New

Growing vegetables—it is only with much hard work and careful watering that the Hong Kong soil can be made to produce good crops.

Territories manages to provide nearly half the vegetables eaten in the colony, and well over half the poultry.

There has also often been a water problem. Hong Kong has no rivers, natural lakes or underground water. Although the average rainfall is about 88 inches (2,240 millimeters), some years bring much less than half the average. Also, most of the rain comes during the summer even in a good year, so the winters are usually dry and sometimes there are droughts. Winter is, nevertheless, the season when many of the food crops are grown. Water storage schemes are gradually solving this problem, but Hong Kong still has to import some of its water from the mainland.

Like their town-dwelling neighbors, Hong Kong farmers are also troubled from time to time by typhoons. Typhoons are storms which bring tremendously heavy rain, and winds which blow at over 100 miles (161 kilometers) an hour. They destroy buildings, wreck ships, flood low-lying areas and, of course, do great damage to farmland and crops. Sometimes lives are lost, too, and a typhoon nearly always leaves some people injured.

Typhoons are a regular feature of summer in the China Sea, but most of them by-pass Hong Kong. However, they often come close enough to cause spells of very wet and windy weather. For the rest of summer, the weather is usually hot and humid, with temperatures sometimes rising above 90 degrees Fahrenheit (32 degrees Celsius), and with an average of seven hours' sunshine a day.

Winter brings a steady, cooling land wind called the winter monsoon. This is usually a dry wind, so there is still plenty of

18

Fresh vegetables being sold at Tai Po Market in the New Territories.

sunshine. But even when the sky is cloudy the weather is never very cold. During the day, the temperature is usually above 50 degrees Fahrenheit (10 degrees Celsius), and often well above 60 degrees Fahrenheit (15.5 degrees Celsius). Frosts are very rare, even in the highest parts of the New Territories.

Although its winters are too cool to give it a true tropical climate, Hong Kong is certainly a tropical country. It lies a little less than 100 miles (161 kilometers) south of the Tropic of Cancer. Visitors know that they have reached the Tropics when they see some of the fruits which Hong Kong farmers grow—bananas, for instance, and pineapples, custard-apples, guavas and papayas (paw-paws). They can also grow many kinds of vegetable all the year round, though the main vegetable crops are grown in the winter months.

Because so much of the land cannot be used for farming or building, there is still plenty of room for wild plants, which make good use of it. Among them are some bright and beautiful tropical flowers, as well as bushes which produce a wide variety of fruits

19

Learning Resources Center
University of Wyoming Libraries
Laramie, WY 82070

As well as the 343 different kinds of wild bird to be found in the colony, domesticated ducks like these are a familiar sight in Hong Kong.

and berries—even wild bananas, wild persimmons and wild kumquats. A kumquat is a small fruit rather like an orange, but visitors who do not know exactly what to look for would be wise to leave the wild ones on the bush—Hong Kong has another wild plant whose fruit is rather like a small orange, but that one is highly poisonous.

As might be expected in a very small country with a very big human population, wild animals are not very plentiful. However, it is still possible to see barking deer, macaque and rhesus monkeys, scaly anteaters, wild pigs and, more rarely, red foxes and leopard cats. There may even be a few true leopards and a tiger or two in

20

the wilder mountain areas, although nobody has seen a leopard since 1957, or a tiger since 1947.

Because so many of Hong Kong's wild animals have been dying out, they are now protected by a law which generally forbids hunting. So too are its 343 different kinds of wild bird. However, there are some varieties of wildlife which manage to thrive, and seem not at all likely to die out. One is the wild pig, which does great damage to crops. It now exists in such large numbers that farmers may be allowed to shoot some in the winter months. Another is a giant snail, usually about five inches (12 centimeters) long. As the ordinary snail is only about one quarter of that length, you can imagine what damage the giants can do to the market gardens which provide Hong Kong with about half of its vegetables. Like a very large part of the human population, the giant snail is an immigrant to Hong Kong.

Although Hong Kong was until recently a British colony, very few of its five and a half million people are British. Only about 26,000 come from Britain itself, while about 20,000 come from other countries in the Commonwealth. Of the remainder, all but about 60,000 are of the Chinese race—that is, about 98 percent of the population. The rest are immigrants from China and from Chinese communities in other parts of Asia.

In thinking of China, we must remember that it is a huge and very ancient country, and that the Chinese nation includes people of many kinds. They differ from each other in appearance, in character, in customs and in language. These differences are clear among the Chinese people of Hong Kong. For example, if you move around a little you should hear at least five quite different Chinese languages being spoken.

That can cause some problems, but they are rarely very serious ones. The great majority of Hong Kong Chinese speak Cantonese, the language of the province around the city of Canton. So people in Hong Kong who speak another Chinese language often learn to speak Cantonese, too.

Even if they do not, they can still understand what Cantonese-speakers write or print. The letters of the huge Chinese alphabet are mainly ideograms—or pictures, if you like. Each stands for a particular thing or a particular idea, not for a particular sound. So if you should see the ideogram for *people* you could safely read "people," even though you know none of the Chinese words for "people." This means that a Hong Kong businessman who speaks only Cantonese and a customer who speaks only Shanghainese can

These trains on the waterfront carry advertisements in both Chinese and English. Each ideogram stands for a single object or idea.

write letters to each other without misunderstandings, and that both can read the same books and newspapers as a neighbor who speaks only Mandarin.

Besides, if they should wish to have a conversation, they could probably get along quite happily in English. English is an official language in Hong Kong. Many Hong Kong Chinese speak it very well, and it has been taught to all children in Chinese-speaking schools from their second primary year.

Now let us look more closely at how, and why, nearly six million people who are mainly Chinese lived for so long under British rule in a very small corner of coastal China.

2

A Million Lights Shall Shine

Early in the thirteenth century, just a year or two before King John of England signed the Magna Carta, the great empire of China was invaded. The invaders were Mongols, fierce, horse-riding nomadic warriors from a region to the north. Their aim was to conquer the whole empire, and they did so, but very slowly. It took them nearly seventy years.

Towards the end of that time, the Emperor of China had little left of his country except the far southeast. He fled there, and died on the Kowloon Peninsula, opposite the island that is now called Hong Kong. Then his brother, still only a boy, rallied the Chinese army for a last battle. They met the Mongols in the area now called the New Territories, and were badly beaten.

After the battle, the boy Emperor and most of the Chinese survivors fled even further south, towards what is now Vietnam. The others crossed the water to Lantau Island. You can meet some of their descendants among the people—mainly farmers, fishermen and Buddhist monks—who live on Lantau today.

The survivors chose Lantau Island rather than Hong Kong Island mainly because Lantau was more populated. In fact, Hong Kong Island was hardly settled at all. It did not even have a name. The few fairly primitive inhabitants lived mainly by fishing, a little farming, and piracy. A harbor on the seaward side was the main haunt of the pirates. It had the Chinese name Heung Kong, which means "Fragrant Water." The water is not very fragrant today, and the harbor is no longer called Heung Kong. It now has the very British name Aberdeen, while the name Heung Kong–spelt Hong Kong, as the first British settlers pronounced it–has become the name of the whole island.

Unlike Hong Kong Island, the area now called Kowloon and the New Territories had long been settled and civilized when the fleeing

These Hakka women live in a walled village near Yuen Long. They are the descendants of a group of people who lived in Kowloon and the New Territories long before the Cantonese came there from China.

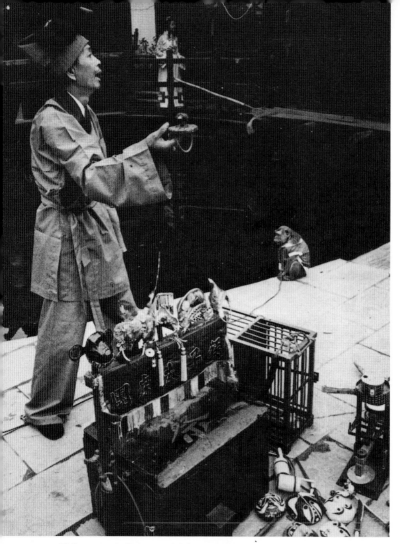

This entertainer and his monkeys perform in the market-place of a replica Sung Dynasty village. The clothing, background and type of entertainment all date from the time of the boy Emperor.

Chinese Emperor arrived in Kowloon. Indeed, he may have chosen it as a place of refuge because he was related to the Tang family, an important Chinese clan who had moved there two centuries earlier, and owned much of the land. In the New Territories, there are still some ancient villages where everybody's surname is Tang.

Kowloon and the New Territories were then part of the Chinese province called Kwangtung (Guangdong), or Canton. So it is not surprising to know that the Tang clan were Cantonese—nor that other Cantonese held neighboring villages when the fleeing Emperor came. There were also at least three quite different groups of people, each with its own way of life and its own language. They were the Hakka, the Hoklo and the Tanka. All three groups were in the area before the first Cantonese, sharing it only with such doubtful neighbors as elephants and crocodiles. All three are still represented there.

This means that Kowloon and the New Territories, with a usable area of only about 100 square miles (259 square kilometers) must have been quite thickly populated centuries before they became part of a British colony. Yet nobody seemed very interested in trying to use Hong Kong Island, barely one mile (1.6 kilometers) across the water from Kowloon. However, there was one person who believed that the island had a future. During the Mongol invasion, a man very famous for his wisdom came to Kowloon and said, "That nameless island may be empty and unwanted now, but I see a time when a million lights shall shine there."

Hong Kong Island had to wait nearly seven hundred years for that prophecy to come true. Even when Britain took it over as a colony, many British people could see no hope for it. One of Queen Victoria's chief ministers called it "a bare island with hardly a house upon it, obviously useless for trade." And a writer of the time produced a book-chapter with this heading: "Hong Kong: Its Position, Prospects, Character and *Utter Worthlessness* from Every Point of View for England."

Those people, and many others who spoke in the same way, were describing a place which became one of the main trading centers in the world and, for its size, one of the richest parts of the British Empire.

Meanwhile, over the centuries after the Mongol invasion, foreign trade was enriching and developing the Chinese city of Canton, on the Pearl River, 90 miles (145 kilometers) from Hong Kong. After the year 1513, the foreign traders were mainly Europeans. By 1557, the Portuguese had a settled trading-center at Macau, on the western side of the very wide river-mouth, about 50 miles (80 kilometers) from Canton.

The traders of other European nations were not willing to be kept at such a distance from the city. In 1715 the British were allowed to set up a factory in Canton itself, on the waterfront. This was not a factory which made goods. It was a great store-house for goods bought in China and goods brought to China for sale. It was also a living-place for the traders and their British employees.

Other foreign traders also set up factories on the Canton waterfront. Near the end of the eighteenth century there were thirteen. And some of the traders were in trouble—especially the

Seven hundred years before this photo of Hong Kong was taken a wise man saw the bare island and predicted that "a million lights shall shine there."

British. From the Chinese, the British could buy great quantities of tea, silk and many other goods that were needed or much wanted in Britain. But Britain produced very little that the Chinese would buy in return. So the British traders were often very short of money to pay for their shiploads of tea and silk.

The only way to solve their problem was an unlawful one—to bring in shiploads of opium from India. Opium is a drug made from the milky juice of poppies. It is useful as a medicine but can be very dangerous. Once people have begun to take it they usually find that they cannot give it up; they become addicted to it. And it does great harm both to their minds and their bodies.

In spite of these dangers, opium was becoming very popular in

29

China. So the government had forbidden traders to bring it in. But the British, and some others, were so desperate for trade goods that they began to smuggle opium, and sell it to Chinese merchants who were willing to break the law.

That was all very well while the merchants could bribe government officers to "keep their eyes closed." The foreign traders were soon getting more money for their smuggled opium than they were paying the Chinese for tea and silks. But then a new viceroy (representative of the Chinese Emperor) was sent to Canton. Viceroy Lin was determined to stop the trade in opium—or "foreign mud," as he and his officers called it. He began by threatening the death penalty to anybody who was caught using it; and he ordered everybody who had any opium—including the foreign traders—to hand it over. He also wanted the traders to sign a bond agreeing that they could be put to death if they brought any more opium to China.

At first, the British traders refused to do either. But by now the British government had its own representative in Canton, and he ordered them to hand over their opium. At the same time he forbade them to sign the bond, or to buy any trade goods from the Chinese for the time being.

Viceroy Lin answered by imprisoning the whole British community in their factories. They were shut up for six weeks, and then told to leave Canton. They went, but only as far as the Portuguese settlement at Macau. That was not enough for Viceroy Lin. The British had hardly made themselves comfortable in Macau when he asked the Portuguese to expel them, and sent soldiers to see that his request was carried out.

Even now, the British were unwilling to leave China. Instead, using about fifty sailing-ships, they crossed the mouth of the Pearl River and sailed as far as the vast harbor between Kowloon and Hong Kong Island. There, they lay uneasily at anchor while they waited for British warships to come and protect them.

By the time warships came, fighting with the Chinese had already started. It went on for two years, with breaks while the two sides tried to satisfy each other and failed. But by then the Chinese could see that they were losing more than they were likely to gain. And the British could see other nations taking all the benefits of trade with China. So the fighting stopped, and peaceful trading began again, with Britain given a tiny part of China—Hong Kong Island—as a permanent and independent trading-base.

Not everyone agreed that Britain had the best of the bargain. There were many who supported the claim that the island was "utterly worthless," and the early years of the colony did little to change their minds. On two occasions nearly all the new buildings were destroyed by typhoons. The market-place was destroyed by fire. Deadly fever epidemics killed many of the people, and drove others away. And the traders were much less prosperous than they had been in Canton. Instead of dealing through Hong Kong, British merchant ships were going direct to seaports on the mainland to unload their cargoes and take on new ones.

Because of all that, a new expression came into the English language during the 1840s. If someone was being especially troublesome or irritating, his victim would say, "Oh, go to Hong

A Chinese opera-singer in costume—opera is just one item of culture which the Chinese brought to Hong Kong.

Kong," meaning "I wish you were as far away from me as possible, in the most unpleasant place possible."

However, people kept coming to Hong Kong for other reasons, especially the Chinese from Canton; and most of those who came were glad to stay. At the end of the 1840s, the colony had about 30,000 people, less than 1,000 of them from countries outside China.

By then, more ships were using the port. More trade was coming with them. And although there was another small war between China and Britain in the 1850s, its only effect on the colony was a useful one. After the war Hong Kong was no longer only an island. It had gained a piece of the mainland, the waterside city of Kowloon. Now it had control of all the sheltered water between—

one of the best harbors in the world. For nearly a hundred years, Hong Kong depended almost entirely on that harbor to earn its living.

It was now beginning to seem possible that the ancient prophecy might come true. The lights that shone from Hong Kong were still far fewer than a million. But its population had doubled and then doubled again between 1850 and 1860. Over those years, many people in China were unsettled and insecure after an unsuccessful rebellion against the Emperor and his government. They saw Hong Kong as a place where they might have better lives without going far from China and the Chinese way of living.

Over the next forty years, thousands of others followed them. Then, right at the end of the century, Hong Kong gained 100,000 new citizens in a single day. Through an agreement between the governments of Britain and China, the 374 square miles (969 square kilometers) of China that are now called the New Territories were added to Hong Kong. And, of course, the people who lived on the land went with it. The transfer was not a gift—just a loan for

Country quiet in the New Territories—can it be preserved?

a period of ninety-nine years, and the ninety-nine years would end in 1997.

The people of the New Territories had hardly settled down as citizens of Hong Kong when there was another rebellion in China. Its leader was the famous Dr. Sun Yat Sen, who had studied medicine in Hong Kong. This time, the rebellion was successful. It made China a republic, with Dr. Sun Yat Sen as president. But its main effect on Hong Kong was to bring in yet more immigrants from China. The population kept growing until the Second World War struck Hong Kong, when it numbered over 1,500,000.

Then, for the first time in the colony's history, the population decreased sharply. Japan attacked and took over the colony in December 1941. The Japanese imprisoned all the British residents whom its soldiers could capture. The rest, and many Chinese too, crossed to Macau and China as refugees. Then, when food grew scarce, the Japanese forced tens of thousands more Chinese to leave. By the end of the war, Hong Kong had lost about one million people.

However, they were very quick to come back when the Japanese left, and nearly a million new immigrants soon followed them. These were people who did not wish to stay in China after it became a Communist country; and refugees from Communist China continued coming to Hong Kong. So too did refugees from other Asian countries where there have been political troubles, including some of the Vietnamese "boat people" who fled from Vietnam by sea, and were much in the international news during 1979.

The Communist revolution in China did more to Hong Kong

A ferry boat in Hong Kong harbor with the skyline in the background.

than swell its population. It put an end to the colony's traditional way of living. In one way or another, nearly all the people of Hong Kong depended for their living on trade between China and the Western countries. They had been doing so for more than a century. But in 1950 the trading stopped completely. China was supporting an invasion of South Korea by North Korea. To show their disapproval, the Western countries put a ban on all trade with China. As a result, Hong Kong found itself almost totally unemployed, with little hope that trade would thrive again, even when the Korean War ended.

So why is it now among the world's busiest and most prosperous small regions?

3

Hong Kong's Industrial Revolution

If you are faced with a serious difficulty—as Hong Kong was in 1950—you can sit down hoping that someone will help you, or you can stand up and try to help yourself. Hong Kong chose the second way.

It was not easy to do so, because the colony had very little with which it could help itself—hardly any minerals, very few other raw materials, not nearly enough land to produce either food for export, or such raw materials as wool, cotton and rubber. There was only the great harbor, and that seemed to be facing a very slack future when trade between China and the Western countries stopped.

However, since ships from half the world had been using Hong Kong harbor to unload Western factory products for sale in China, they could also unload factory machines and raw materials for use in Hong Kong; with those, Hong Kong could perhaps get over its difficulty. It could try to make and export its own industrial goods

Unloading a freighter by lighter in Hong Kong harbor.

instead of merely trading in industrial goods made by other people.

That is exactly what happened in the years after 1950. Without any government money, equipment, buildings or training the people of Hong Kong learned how to make and market things which millions of foreigners wanted. They turned the colony into a busy and prosperous industrial country.

Often—like the man who began a successful plastic flower industry—they had to teach themselves. By the 1950s, plastics had proved just how widely they could replace more expensive materials such as metals, cotton, wood, paper, glass and clay. In the United States, artificial flowers molded in plastic had become very

Unloading containers.

popular, and were being sold by the millions. When one of those plastic flowers arrived in Hong Kong, a local businessman saw its possibilities. He imported a supply of the petrochemical with which plastic flowers are made, taught himself how to make them and, before long, had a factory shipping them to the United States and other overseas markets. There, they could be sold at less than half the price of plastic flowers made in other countries, and still give the Hong Kong factory a good profit.

In fact, they gave such a good profit that the first factory soon had rivals competing for a share of the export market, and now there are over 400 factories making plastic flowers. About 4,500 more make plastic goods of all kinds, from furniture and floor tiles to water pipes and pencil sharpeners. Hong Kong factories also make the machines and molds that are used in the plastics industry, and export some of these to other plastic-making countries.

About 90,000 people are employed in making plastics, but that

Scene in a Hong Kong tailor's shop.

seems a very small number compared to the work force of another industry which grew very quickly during the 1950s—the making of cloth and clothes. More than half of the colony's 900,000 industrial workers spin yarn, weave cloth, or make clothing. Their products account for nearly half the cargoes that now leave Hong Kong harbor. In Britain today, many employees of the Houses of Parliament are wearing officially provided Hong Kong shirts. The label *Made in Hong Kong* has become a familiar one not only on jeans and sweaters but also on more expensive and formal clothes.

The Hong Kong factory-workers themselves usually wear clothing of the Western type, both for work and for leisure. So do most other people who live and work in towns. However, some elders still prefer traditional Chinese clothes. Also, women of most ages like to wear the *cheongsam*—a long elegant, fairly tight-fitting dress with the sides slit from ankle to knee. In this form, the *cheongsam* is a fairly modern invention. The real, traditional *cheongsam* was quite a different garment—and much less stylish. Nowadays, *cheongsams* of the older type are more likely to be seen in farming and fishing villages than in city areas as are other traditional everyday clothes, including the enormous straw hats that appear so often in pictures.

Unlike the start of the plastics industry, there was nothing of the teach-yourself method about the early days of cloth-making and clothes-making. But there was a stroke of good luck. In China, the years before the Communist revolution were a time of unrest, uncertainty and civil war. Industry was suffering badly, and many factory-owners believed that conditions would grow worse for them

Shopping for clothes at the famous Stanley Market.

if the Communists took over. Some of them decided to move to Hong Kong. They arrived not long before China became a Communist country, bringing their machines, their raw materials and even some skilled workers with them. That was just what Hong Kong needed. Less than a year later came the ban on trade with China, and the migrant factory-owners were ready to give thousands of unemployed Hong Kong people a new way to earn a living.

Manufacturers in countries much further away than China also had a hand in Hong Kong's industrial revolution. To them, the colony seemed an ideal place in which to open overseas branches. Taxes were very low. Nearly everything else could be imported or exported without payment of duties. Import and export shipping could rely on a first-class harbor. Factory space could be obtained cheaply. There were large markets handy in the countries of southeast Asia and the Pacific. And there were plenty of skillful, hard-working, intelligent people ready to take jobs at wages which were fairly low by Western standards.

40

This girl is testing electronic machines made in another factory.

Those advantages soon brought overseas companies into the developing industrial life of Hong Kong, especially from Britain, the United States, Australia and Japan. They work mainly in engineering and electronics, and have helped to put Hong Kong among the world's largest exporters of transistor radios, computer parts and digital watches.

However, less than 500 of the colony's 46,000 factories are owned by overseas companies. The others have all been developed and made successful by Hong Kong people, using their own skills, energy and money.

Nor does all the colony's industrial work go on in those 46,000 factories. If you visit a Hong Kong family you are likely to find that their home—usually a very small and simple one—looks more like a workshop than a living-place. The whole family may be making toys, umbrellas or any one of a hundred small products on their own account. Or else they may be working on any of a hundred others that have been made in a factory and then sent to home-workers for assembling or finishing. Through the thin walls which separate this

41

Learning Resources Center
University of Wyoming Libraries
Laramie, WY 82070

family from their neighbors, you can hear the tools and machines of other families busy at the same tasks. You may be disturbed by these noises at any hour of the night. Hong Kong's home-workers are hard workers; they do not take much notice of clocks.

Of course, the working hours are much shorter—and the working conditions much better—in the proper factories. However, there are some things about Hong Kong factory work which would certainly surprise a Western worker. For example, there are no fixed working hours for men over 17 years old. They can be kept on the job as long as they are willing or able to stay, and they have a working week of six full days. Indeed, it was not until 1977 that employers were obliged by law to give them one rest day a week. Even the workers who have fixed hours—women, and young people aged between 15 and 17—work the full six-day week.

Hong Kong workers also have few holidays. True, they have days off for the Chinese New Year and other Chinese festivals as well as some public holidays, but their paid annual leave is limited to seven days. Even that is a fairly recent benefit. Before the British Government made a new law in 1976, they had no paid annual leave at all. The same new law made it easier for them to have paid sick leave. It also improved conditions in factories where the work might be injurious to health or safety.

As for wages, many Hong Kong workers are paid in a way which has long been frowned upon by Western trade unions. They earn their money not from the amount of time that they spend on the job, but from the amount of work that they do in the time. This means that the quickest workers earn the highest wages. Trade

Hong Kong workers are paid in Hong Kong dollars like these.

unions think that this is not very fair to people who work as hard as they can, but are unable to keep up the pace. They also dislike the possibility that it will leave all workers without enough money to live on when there is not much work for them to do.

Some Hong Kong workers are paid in a way that is even less pleasing to trade unions. Instead of dealing direct with an employer, workers offer their services to an agent called a *compradore*. The compradore chooses those who are willing to work for the lowest pay, and then sells their labor at the highest wage he can persuade the employer to give. The difference, of course, is the compradore's profit—and it can be a very good profit indeed when there are many unemployed people competing for work.

43

All that may suggest that the lot of the Hong Kong worker is not a very happy one. But in fact his pay and conditions are generally better than those of workers in most other Asian countries. Both pay and conditions are steadily improving as industries grow more prosperous, and as the government gets more involved in looking after the interests of workers. They would perhaps improve even more if the trade union movement were stronger. However, the unions often seem to be more concerned with politics than with the welfare of workers, and there is a good deal of disunity and dissension among them.

Even if the unions were more united and active, there would be little for them to do in many factories. One out of ten factories in Hong Kong are so small that there is something of a family feeling about them. Employers and employees are usually in close personal touch with each other, and can very often settle disputes and grievances among themselves. Besides, many employers need no encouragement in trying to make workers contented. They look after their employees very well, often giving them benefits in addition to the value of their wages. Among these are pay for the weekly rest day, free lodgings, cheap meals and a bonus equal to a full month's wages at the time of the Chinese New Year holiday.

Now that we have seen something of working conditions in modern Hong Kong, shall we find out how living conditions compare with them?

4

Living in Hong Kong

Even if their own cities are very crowded, visitors are usually astonished to find so many people living so close to their neighbors in Hong Kong. Very few of them live in houses. Their homes are mainly small apartments or single rooms, sometimes in modern high-rise blocks, sometimes in blocks that are not so modern, sometimes in tenement buildings that are not modern at all, but old, unsanitary and rather ramshackle. Large families often cram themselves into these small areas. Also, many families happily add to the congestion by letting part of a room to another family, or by using it as a workshop or a small factory as well as a living-place. Some even double their floor-space by rigging up a flimsy extra floor between the real floor and the ceiling, to make room for another family or two.

The shanty-town of Wah Fu—built of packing-cases and driftwood.

A visitor need not go inside to find out how crowded the buildings are. He can tell by the noise that comes from them, and by the washing that is always flapping on poles lashed to their window-frames and balconies.

In most cases, all this over-crowding is not because the people are too poor to afford more space around them. Some prefer to spend as little as they can on rent, and use their money for other things—perhaps for developing a small factory or business, or for joining the fast-growing number of car-owners. The majority live so tightly packed together because the population is growing much faster than the speed at which the government and private landlords can put up buildings to house it. If people are not prepared to pack into a block of very small apartments or a honeycombed tenement building, they must live in a shanty-town, or put up a rough shelter for themselves on a roof or in whatever empty space they can find. There, unless they go well out of the cities, they will be just as crowded.

Shanty-towns began to spread around the cities of Hong Kong after the Second World War, when refugees from China began flooding in. They were built of old iron sheeting, canvas, sacks, packing cases—anything that the refugees could find or buy cheaply. The buildings were not all "houses." Many of the refugees were skilled people, who brought their tools and machines and work materials with them. They soon set up shanty workshops and even shanty factories.

In the early 1950s, perhaps a million people were living in shanty-towns and other makeshift accommodations. They had no lavatories, no piped water, no electricity, no conveniences of any kind. They could not expect such things, because they were squatters, living where they had no right to be. While they lived like this they were in constant danger—from disease and from fire. So were the many other people to whom the disease and fire might have spread.

At the end of Christmas Day 1953 there was a very serious fire. It destroyed a whole shanty-town, leaving 50,000 people without even packing-cases to live in. The government then decided that it must do something before an even worse disaster occurred. It began a building program designed to provide cleaner, safer, more comfortable homes for the squatters and for thousands of other people who were very badly housed.

This program is still going on, and so far it has been very

Blocks of low-cost housing built by the government of Hong Kong to accommodate people who once lived in shanty-town.

successful. Many of the high-rise buildings which form Hong Kong's city skyline are blocks of apartments and rooms housing people who were once squatters in shanty-towns. Altogether, more than two million people have their homes in buildings put up by the government, but the number of those living in shanty-towns is still over 700,000.

That may seem a high figure, but the government must spread its money very carefully. Unlike some countries which are no longer British colonies but still draw money from Britain, Hong Kong supports itself: it even paid three-quarters of the cost of keeping British armed forces in the colony prior to 1997.

The money for this—and for all the works and services which the government must provide—comes mainly from taxes of various kinds and from lotteries. As tax rates are very low compared to those of most Western countries, the government could hardly build housing more quickly without borrowing more money than it could hope to pay back.

Nor is there enough money to provide all the education, health and social welfare services which people in Britain and some other Western countries expect from their governments. Education in Hong Kong is free and compulsory for six years in a primary school and three in a secondary school. Ninety percent of the children go on to higher levels of secondary education. Almost one-fourth will go on to university level education. Those who wish to stay at school usually have to pay, either in a government school, or in one of the many private schools where fees are much higher. However, there are free places for some

Primary school children in their classroom—education in Hong Kong is free and compulsory for nine years.

students in the higher forms of government secondary schools. There are also grants or loans for further education at the University of Hong Kong, the Chinese University of Hong Kong, the Hong Kong Polytechnic or at one of the four teacher training colleges.

Hong Kong's education authorities have the same problem as people looking for somewhere to live–there are not enough buildings to go round. Because of this, most schools fit two school days into one. Half the pupils begin their school day at eight o'clock in the morning and end it at one o'clock in the afternoon. Then the other half take over for a school day which ends in the early evening, at half-past six.

This causes some problems when it comes to fitting games and other outdoor activities into school timetables, but the schools seem to manage very well. Naturally enough for people who live close to the sea, swimming and water games are very popular. Hong Kong children can also be seen playing most of the other sports that are played in Western countries. They have their own Chinese games, too, and a Chinese system of physical training called Tai Chi. Tai Chi is not only for children. Many adults keep to it all their lives, and people of all ages can often be seen doing Tai Chi exercises in parks, on beaches, in alleyways between buildings, or wherever they can find room to move their arms and legs freely.

On school holidays and on public holidays, children can also take part in sporting events, camps and classes organized by the Department of Education's Recreation and Sport Service. This service is for adults as well as for children, and many of its

The child on the right in this picture is giving the traditional greeting for the Chinese New Year. Both children are dressed in traditional clothes.

Performing the Chinese ribbon dance at a theater restaurant in Kowloon.

projects are family affairs.

Indoors, music and dancing seem to be the favorite activities among Hong Kong children, both at school and in their spare time. They play Chinese and Western music on Chinese and Western instruments, and well over 30,000 young performers can be heard at the annual Schools Music Festival. Some of them have even taken their talents abroad. Among these are the Hong Kong Children's Choir and several school dance teams, who have made international tours and performed in international festivals. In 1982 Hong Kong held its first Children's Arts Festival at the new 19-story Hong Kong Arts Center.

School health generally is looked after by the government. Any

Learning Resources Center
University of Wyoming Libraries
Laramie, WY 82070

individual child can have as much free medical treatment as he needs if his parents make a small annual payment to the School Medical Service. The payment is really very small but surprisingly few parents take advantage of it. Only about one sixth of the 1,400,000 schoolchildren are enrolled.

However, they can receive very cheap medical treatment in another way, and so can their parents. Hong Kong does not have a National Health Service but throughout the region there are about four hundred medical clinics, and at some of these a patient can receive treatment very cheaply. There are also floating clinics for the people who live on some of the smaller islands, while flying doctors travel by helicopter to treat patients in other remote areas and perhaps bring them back to the hospital.

The government runs only thirteen of the forty-four hospitals in Hong Kong, but twenty of the others are helped with government money. In these, as well as in the hospitals run by the government, patients have to pay very little, and sometimes nothing at all.

Medical treatment generally is in the modern Western manner and Hong Kong's hospitals are among the finest and best equipped in the world. But many Hong Kong people still prefer the traditional Chinese methods and medicines. These include acupuncture—the needle treatment that has become popular abroad—as well as medicines with such unlikely ingredients as snake's bile and monkey's liver. Other parts of the snake are used, too, both in medicines and in food, so it is quite easy to buy

Pavilions and flowers in Tiger Balm Gardens.

a live snake in Hong Kong. Just ask someone to show you the way to a snake shop.

Even if they do not use traditional Chinese medicines, Hong Kong people are reminded of one every time they pass or go for a stroll in the famous Tiger Balm Gardens. Tiger Balm is an ointment which, so its Chinese inventor said, will cure practically any pain. So many people in and out of China used it and were satisfied by it that the inventor became a multi-millionaire. He was also a very generous man, who spent more than half his Tiger Balm money on gifts and benefits to the public. His gift to the people of Hong Kong was the Tiger Balm Gardens.

Some people in Hong Kong cannot afford Tiger Balm, or even the small fees charged by the government medical clinics, and these may claim public assistance allowances from the government's Social Welfare Department. Public assistance may also be claimed by people who are in need for any reason—but only if they are genuinely in need through no fault of their own.

53

There are, however, no general unemployment benefits, pensions or family allowances.

Disaster victims too are looked after by the Social Welfare Department—and disasters seem to happen fairly often in Hong Kong. In one recent year, eighty-seven disasters put about 13,000 people in need of assistance. Among the worst were a landslide which partly destroyed a block of apartments and shops, and a fire which burnt out one of the remaining shanty-towns, leaving over 3,000 more people in need of homes.

The money which the government spends on social welfare comes partly from the sale of tickets in lotteries. Lotteries and other forms of gambling have always been very popular among the Chinese, who are great believers in luck. So as long as the Hong Kong Chinese can afford to buy lottery tickets, they can be sure that their needy neighbors will have some help.

However, the help that comes from lotteries and other government money is fairly limited, so there is plenty of room for work by private charities. Much of this is done by religious bodies, who also run some of the hospitals and schools.

As so many Hong Kong people are Chinese, it is not surprising to find that the main religions of Hong Kong are the ancient faiths of China, particularly Confucianism, Buddhism and Taoism. Next to those two faiths, Christianity is the most favored. Including European residents, the Christian population totals about half a million.

There are also some Hindus, Jews and Muslims. The Hindus and some of the Muslims are migrants from India and Pakistan,

The Buddhist monastery and richly decorated new temple on Lantau Island.

while the Jews have come from many countries. Some of the Jewish families have been in Hong Kong for more than a century, and have played a very important part in its development. One of these families, the Kadoories, made a great deal of money in the colony's trading days and then gave much of it to the government, to be used for making loans to farmers. Money from the Kadoories has also helped a large number of refugees to settle on farms in the New Territories, and to found an experimental farm.

The Jewish community is so small that it needs only one synagogue—a very impressive one provided by another famous family of the trading days: the Sassoons. However, there are about six hundred Christian churches, and even more temples for followers of the Chinese religions. Many of these temples as well as many shops and houses display statues of a great and confusing variety of gods and goddesses. The variety makes sense only if we understand that Buddhists and Taoists regard the statues in much the same way as some Christians regard statues of their saints.

Not unnaturally, for a people who live near the sea and depend so much on the sea, the most popular of the gods and goddesses is T'ien Hou—or Tin Hau, as the name is sometimes spelled. T'ien Hou is the patron goddess of sailors and travelers. If you come to a Hong Kong haven that is used by seafarers or fishermen, you are almost certain to find a T'ien Hou temple somewhere along the shore. Rather more surprisingly, you will also find a few well away from the waterfront. They have lost their place by the sea because land has been reclaimed.

T'ien Hou's birthday is marked by special services and celebrations at the temples, and fishermen decorate their boats with banners and signal flags. Some other traditional Chinese festivals are much more widespread. One of them—the Chinese New Year Festival—spreads widely in time as well as in place. Most people stop work for four days and the celebrations go on for another ten. These are days for buying new clothes, family visits and present-giving. Children with large numbers of adult

Dragon boats decorated for the festival.

relatives can do very well out of the festivities. The relatives are expected to give them presents of money, called lucky money.

Like T'ien Hou's birthday, the New Year celebrations are connected with old Chinese religious traditions. So too are most of the other Chinese festivals in Hong Kong, even Tuen Ng, the famous Dragon Boat Festival. Dragon boats are huge open canoes up to 100 feet (30 meters) long, decorated with dragon figureheads. During the festival, crews of about fifty men paddle them furiously in races which are supposed to look like a battle among dragons, while drums are beaten loudly and excited spectators try to make more noise than the drums. The

Musicians dressed in traditional costume at the Hung Shing Festival.

spectators also eat the traditional Dragon Festival food, flavored rice cooked in a wrapping of lotus leaves.

To the visitor, the festival seems no more than a happy and very energetic sporting event. But to those who know Chinese religious traditions, the race has a very serious purpose. It is meant to stir up a fight among some real dragons who live in the heavens, because fights among those dragons cause rain to fall.

There are other explanations of the festival, including one which says that it is held in memory of some rowers who used their oars to frighten hungry fish away from the body of a drowned hero, while other people threw rice parcels into the water to entice the fish away. However, the dragon explanation seems to be the oldest, and is no less likely than any of the others.

All the traditional Chinese festivals are dated by the old Chinese calendar, which means that their dates on the Western calendar change from year to year. It also means that—except in the very rare years when the Chinese New Year begins on January 1st—Hong Kong people are lucky enough to have two New Year's Day public holidays.

At the time of the dragon boat races, visitors who are more interested in horses than in boats can see the last events of the Hong Kong horse-racing season. Hong Kong people like horse races—and the gambling that goes with them. There are race meetings on most public holidays over the nine months from September to June, and also on some evenings. One of the most important is held on a day that was a public holiday throughout

Hong Kong's racecourse.

the British Empire in Queen Victoria's time, but is now an ordinary workday for most people, even in Britain itself, the Queen's Birthday. However, Hong Kong still celebrates the day with a public holiday. The birthday ceremonies and festivities remind the visitor that Queen Elizabeth of England, Wales, and Scotland, was also until recently the Queen of Hong Kong.

Until the turnover of Hong Kong to China, the Queen's representative in Hong Kong—the Governor—was the head of the colony's government, and responsible to the Parliament of the United Kingdom. The body which made laws and did other parliamentary work was called the Legislative Council. The Council's sixty (originally forty-eight) members were appointed by the Governor, usually from among prominent Hong Kong citizens. In 1991 elections for one-third of the seats were held for the first time and in 1995 elections for all the seats were held.

There was also a smaller body, called the Executive Council, whose job was to advise the Governor, and help him with its special knowledge of Hong Kong and its affairs.

At midnight on June 30, 1997 the British flag was lowered for the last time and Hong Kong became a Special Administrative Region of the People's Republic of China. The Chinese had appointed a Preparatory Committee, which included many prominent Hong Kong citizens, to set up a governing framework for the territory. For the present, a Chief Executive (generally a Hong Kong businessman) will be appointed by the Chinese government. A 400-member Selection Committee, appointed by the Chinese government, will choose a 60-member Legislative

A farming village in the New Territories.

Council similar to the British one. The Chief Executive and Legislative Council are invisioned as eventually being elected by the people of Hong Kong, but the future of democratic processes in the territory is uncertain.

Most of the people who live in the villages of Hong Kong are mainly farmers, and we have already seen that about 900,000 city-dwellers work in factories. But Hong Kong has over a million other people of working age. What do they do for a living?

5

Earning a Living

Hong Kong's new factory industries not only saved 900,000 people from unemployment. They also provided work for a nearly unemployed harbor. Most of the raw materials used by the factories come in by sea. Most of the goods made in the factories go out by sea. That in itself has made the harbor as busy as it was in the days when most ships brought in Western goods for sale in China and carried Chinese goods away.

After ten years of factory development, Hong Kong's own exports were bringing in as much money as the colony had once earned from buying and re-exporting the products of China, and well before then Chinese goods were coming back again. The ban on trade had lasted less than two years, and Hong Kong gradually returned to its old place as the main center for business between China and the Western countries. Now, China receives about one third of its export earnings from goods that go first to Hong Kong, either by sea or by the Kowloon-Canton railway.

Some of these exports go no further than Hong Kong. China supplies nearly half of what the colony's six million people eat and

Inside a modern shopping mall in Kowloon.

drink—including water. It also supplies the varied stock of traditional and modern goods on sale at the large retail stores which the Chinese government has opened in Hong Kong's crowded shopping centers. Generally, Hong Kong people can afford to buy these more easily than most people in China.

In return, China offers a growing market for some of Hong Kong's own exports—and these are not all factory products. Among them are large quantities of human sewage which the Chinese use to fertilize farmlands. This export adds the equivalent of about two million American dollars each year to Hong Kong's income. In a tiny country so tightly crammed with people, it also helps to solve a very serious sanitary problem.

In one way or another, Hong Kong's huge traffic in exports and imports earns a living for many thousands of people–buyers, sellers, bankers, insurance agents, seamen, railwaymen, truck drivers, dock workers, clerks, police. This was the colony's traditional work. Among the leading buyers and sellers there is still one of the firms that began it–the firm of Jardine and Matheson.

Jardine and Matheson or Jardine's as the firm is usually called goes back to the days before Hong Kong became a British colony. It was started in Canton by two Scottish traders, but was driven out during the troubles over smuggled opium. When it settled again on Hong Kong Island it set up a large cannon to protect its waterside warehouse from attacks by sea. And the cannon is still there, pointing across the harbor near the entrance to the underwater road tunnel which now links Hong Kong Island with Kowloon. Visitors who hear it in action need not be alarmed. It is fired (without a cannon ball) as a time-check every day at noon, and also on special occasions, for instance at midnight on December 31st, to welcome the New Year.

In modern times, Jardine's has become much more than a trading firm. It has spread its interests to many of the other industries which help Hong Kong people to earn a living. Among these is aircraft repair. Aircraft repairing may seem an unimportant industry for a country so small that it needs only one airport and has very little air traffic inside its own boundaries, but Hong Kong has made it very important. The airlines of most Asian countries use the Hong Kong repair industry to keep their aircraft in good flying order.

Ship repairing too is a very important industry. So is

64

A hydrofoil in Hong Kong harbor heading towards Lantau Island. Ship-building is an important industry in Hong Kong.

shipbuilding. Both keep many people at work in dry docks and shipyards spread widely along the waterfronts, and many of the ships which they handle are brought over very long distances for repairs and refitting or sometimes for scrapping.

Ship-scrapping was one of the first new industries to begin in Hong Kong after the Second World War. During the war, over a hundred ships were sunk in Hong Kong Harbor. Many of them lay in places where they were a danger to peacetime shipping. And Hong Kong people, who are never slow at spotting opportunities, made the most of clearing them away. They broke them up and re-forged their steel to make reinforcing rods for the building industry.

Thus, many of the skyscrapers which now look down on the harbor are held in place by ships which were once sunk beneath it.

The ship-breaking industry did not die when all the wrecks were used up. All over the world there were, and still are, ships sunk in war action or in ordinary peacetime sailing. Hong Kong breakers have found that they could buy these, bring them back to their yards, and still make a profit from the pieces. Hong Kong, with no iron of its own, is now making steel rods for export as well as for its own building industry.

To the eyes and ears of a visitor, building itself seems to be Hong Kong's biggest industry. It is certainly the most obvious. Everywhere one turns, something old is being noisily knocked down and something new—but ten times as big— noisily put up. Only the more distant farmers seem free from the screeching, thumping, crashing and rattling of builders' machinery. Even some of the fishing people who live on their boats are not clear of noise. Their boats are crammed so tightly, so close to built-up shores, that they hear as much land-noise as people who live in the buildings.

About 34,000 of Hong Kong's people earn a living as fishermen. They do so from about 5,000 boats, mainly Chinese junks—and catch nearly all of the sea-fish eaten in the colony. Most of them live on their boats with their families—and also with their animals and poultry—providing a sight that is much admired and photographed by visitors.

The visitors themselves rank fairly high among the ways in which modern Hong Kong people earn a living. In recent times they have been coming at the rate of over two million every year. And it takes a good many people to provide two million others with accommodations, food, transport, entertainment and souvenirs. In return, the visitors spend their money in Hong Kong–they are the colony's second largest source of foreign income.

Shall we take a closer look at what they see while they are spending it?

Fishing-boats crowded close to the shore at the east end of Hong Kong Island.

6

The Crowded Center

In the 1960s, the Hong Kong government greatly improved the light-buoys and other shipping beacons in Hong Kong Harbor. It had to do so, because there was such a dazzle of land lights on that side of Hong Kong Island that ships' pilots were often in difficulties. They could hardly see the beacons which marked the safe routes and the danger-spots.

The land lights go right up to the top of Mount Victoria, The Peak, as it is usually called, and their spreading dazzle reminds the visitor that full marks must be given to that wise old man who came to Kowloon seven hundred years ago. He was absolutely right when he foretold that a million lights would one day shine from Hong Kong Island. He would have been just as right if he had stood on Hong Kong Island and foretold the same of the Kowloon Peninsula. When a modern visitor looks across to Kowloon from Mount Victoria, he can see another million lights shining there.

The visitor can, and probably will, also go right up Mount Victoria. In fact, he may have to go much of the way to reach the place where he is staying. Almost the whole of the mountainside is

Hong Kong's Harbor and skyline seen from Victoria Peak.

a residential area and for local people it is often a case of "the richer you are, the higher up The Peak you live." However, you can reach the top without owning or hiring one of the shiny big limousines which crowd the island's rocks. A trolley or a bus will do most of the climbing for you, or a 14-seat "maxi-taxi" will take you all the way. You will not pay much in fares, either. They are cheap indeed when judged against public transport charges in Western countries.

On the upper slopes of The Peak, it is hard for a visitor to remember that he is in one of the world's most thickly populated countries. But his memory will need no jogging as he moves down to the lower slopes and the harborside. There, the Central District ribbons along about six miles (ten kilometers) of the island's coastline, looking very modern and European in the streets which lie nearest the harbor, not so modern and very Chinese in the side streets, alleys and flights of steps which lie behind them.

All that ribbon is as closed-in and crowded as the upper slopes of The Peak seem open and roomy. There are even parts of it where—as in most of the schools—the day is divided between two groups of occupants. For example, there is a very large parking area in Rumsey Street, not far from the piers where passengers board ferry-boats for the other islands, or for the Portuguese colony of Macau, on the Pearl River over in China. This area is very convenient for a passenger who comes to his ferry-pier by car, provided that he is back in time to collect the car by early evening. After that, the Rumsey Street parking lot becomes a busy and noisy night market, crammed with stalls at which late shoppers can find and bargain for practically anything that they need and much that they do not need. Hong Kong stall-holders are very good salespeople.

Like Rumsey Street, many other streets in Central and its

A rickshaw—no longer the most familiar sight in Hong Kong traffic.

In the old parts of the city modern motor traffic has not entirely replaced this traditional way of carrying goods—on bamboo poles.

suburbs have names that could be found in the cities of the United Kingdom—such names as Queen's Road, Kennedy Road, Lyndhurst Terrace and Wyndham Street. However, there are also many streets with Chinese names. A visitor could turn off Queen's Road and find himself in Li Yuen Street, or cross Wing Lok Street as he walks from Connaught Road to Bonham Strand through Man Wa Lane. He must sometimes think twice before he can be sure that a Chinese-looking name really is Chinese. For instance, Ho Lei Woo To looks Chinese enough, but in fact it is Chinese only in spelling. The name itself came from Britain by way of the United States; people from those countries spell it Hollywood.

Rather confusingly, our visitor could find himself in other streets which have one name in English and a quite different name in Chinese. A Chinese resident would probably call Wyndham Street Ma Fa Kai (Flower Market Street), while a British resident would be more likely to say Egg Street than Wing Sing Street. There is a practical reason for the rather odd name Egg Street. Eggs are the main items sold in many of the shops. Nor do the egg-dealers stop at the ordinary hen's egg. They can provide a customer with eggs from many kinds of bird, and these eggs are either fresh, preserved, or prepared in a dozen different ways. Of course their wares include the famous hundred-year-old eggs which some Chinese regard as a delicacy although the name should not be taken too seriously. To people who like their eggs fresh, these are certainly very old, but their age should be counted in days, not years.

Wing Sing (or Egg) Street is only a short walk from Wing On or Cloth Street. There, the shops and stalls overflow with cloth of all

72

A view of Jordan Road, Kowloon.

kinds and colors, from many different countries. Hong Kong is a free port. This means that the products of other countries may be brought in without payment of Customs duties, to compete freely with Hong Kong's own products. Nor is there any sales tax or other charge on traders or customers. So visitors from many countries can buy good cloth in Wing On Street much more cheaply than they can buy it at home. They can also have it made very cheaply—almost while they wait—into good quality suits and dresses.

Central has other streets in which most of the shops deal mainly in one particular commodity. In Hillier Street it is live snakes, pickled snakes and even snake poison, which many Chinese like to mix with wine as a winter drink and as a cure for rheumatism. In

73

This camera shop sells the very latest in cameras—but the salesman still have a traditional abacus on the counter for their own use.

Lyndhurst Terrace it is the magnificently embroidered costumes worn by the singers in Chinese operas. In part of the long Queen's Road it is jewelry and jade ornaments—pink, white, brown and several other colors as well as the more common jade green. In Wellington Street it is articles made of ivory, often very delicately carved, and including the small thin ivory slabs used in the popular and very noisy Chinese table game *mah jong*.

Of course most of these articles may also be bought in other streets. So may practically everything else. Nearly everybody in Central seems to be selling something—in a shop, or from a stall, a basket or even a pocket. For all that, Hong Kong people think of

74

Beautifully carved ivory pieces in a Hong Kong shop.

Kowloon on the other side of the harbor as the colony's main shopping center. Central is thought of as the center of government, banking, insurance, international business, entertainment and social life. The main buildings connected with all these activities are clustered in or fairly close to a part of the harborside area called Central District.

The six-mile (10 kilometer) strip of coastland taken up by Central is nowhere more than about one mile (1.6 kilometers) wide. In places, its width narrows to less than one quarter of a mile (0.4 kilometer). Outside that boundary Hong Kong Island is much less thickly-populated, and much less built over. There is even room for some farming. One of the bigger farms—a dairy farm—is worked in a way that surprises many of the visitors who come across it. Instead of driving the cows out to pasture, the farmhands go to

75

Learning Resources Center
University of Wyoming Libraries
Laramie, WY 82070

grassy patches in the hills, cut the grass and carry it down to the cows.

There is also room for the wildlife whose numbers are growing now that the whole of Hong Kong Island is a nature reserve, and for people who live in the densely-packed tall blocks of Central to get out in the open air. Many of them take advantage of it, especially at the fine beaches along the southern coast, and at Ocean Park. Ocean Park is a very large seaside recreation area with a zoo which includes the largest aquarium in the world. The aquarium is built in a way that allows sea creatures to live in their natural conditions. At the same time they are closely observed and very carefully protected. Visitors may look at them from glassed-in galleries as much as twenty feet (six meters) below the surface of the water, and so have a genuine "diver's-eye view" of undersea life.

However, even this side of Hong Kong Island has its crowded corners. The largest is Aberdeen, which lies in a very sheltered position on the coast to the south of The Peak. To a traveler driving in from the road which encircles The Peak, it seems just a growing industrial town that could be yet another suburb of Central. In fact, nearly everyone visiting Hong Kong Island makes a trip out to Aberdeen because it is crowded in a rather unusual way.

7

The Floating People, and Some Others

Aberdeen Harbor is Heung Kong, the ancient fishermen's haven and pirates' haunt that gave Hong Kong its name. Pirates no longer come there—as far as the very efficient Hong Kong police force knows—but the permanent fishing population is now much larger than it was in pirate days. In the 1960s it was larger still, but some

A family aboard their fishing-junk in Aberdeen harbor. The mother is rowing a sampan.

of the fishermen have found that they can make more money by taking jobs in the booming factory industries. Others—mainly younger people—have found that the fishing industry does not need them. With modern fishing methods and equipment, as well as engines instead of sails, boats can now be worked with smaller crews.

However, much of Aberdeen Harbor is still tightly crammed with fishing-boats, mainly the traditional Chinese vessels called junks. And for every boat there is at least one fisherman and his family, as well as a cage of hens. There is probably a dog, too, often in a floating kennel tied to the boat's stern. On many of the boats it would be difficult to find room for a dog to live aboard. The average Hong Kong fishing-craft is not much longer than two medium-sized cars standing end to end; yet it often has to hold a large family with all their household equipment and other belongings, to say nothing of the engine that moves it, the hen-cage, fishing-gear and a day's catch of fish.

Of course, there is nothing unusual about living in a boat. There are boat-dwellers in many countries. To Western eyes, the unusual thing about Aberdeen and Hong Kong's other fishing harbors is that they have so many boats crowded so closely together, and that the people who live in them have so little to do with the land. In fact, it is sometimes said that these people never leave the water until they die. That may be an exaggeration, but it is certainly true that they need not leave it while they are alive. Floating shopkeepers bring them their groceries and other supplies. Floating mailmen deliver their letters. Floating doctors come when they are

Floating shops in Aberdeen harbor.

ill. Their friends who live on land can visit them by floating taxi. If they should want to have a meal away from home, they can row across to a floating restaurant. Their children are taken in rowing-boats to floating schools.

Because so many floating people live so closely together, Aberdeen Harbor no longer deserves its old name Heung Kong, which means Fragrant Water. The water is neither fragrant nor very clean. However, the boats and their floating families are very clean. It would be hard to find more spotless rooms in any house ashore than the tiny, crowded living-quarters of a Hong Kong

79

fishing-boat, or more spotless children than those who come bouncing out of the boats at school time.

These floating families of Hong Kong's fishing harbors are sometimes called boat people, but that name is now confusing. Since 1975, it has also been given to large numbers of refugees from the Communist government of Vietnam, which lies southwest of Hong Kong on the Asian mainland. These Vietnamese were neither fishing people nor boat-dwellers. They were mainly townspeople, but because it was almost impossible to get out of Vietnam by land they left by sea, uncomfortably crowded into old and dangerous boats—hence the name "boat people."

Hong Kong had to watch the numbers of Vietnam boat people very carefully. It was already seriously overcrowded with its own people and with immigrants—legal and illegal—from China. However, it could hardly turn sick and starving people away. There was one boatload who could not have been turned away in any case. They deliberately wrecked their boat, a very large one, on the coast. So Hong Kong made the best of a bad situation, and managed to find homes, some temporary, some permanent, for another surge of uninvited inhabitants.

Not all of Hong Kong's fishing people live on their boats. Some prefer to live on the harborside, in villages of close-packed little houses, often built over the water on stilts. These villages are mainly on the few outlying islands that are comfortable and fertile enough to have populations—such islands as Cheung Chau, Peng Chau, Tsing Yi and Lantau.

Cheung Chau is a busy little island with some small modern

The Bun Festival—the tall pillars are made of buns!

industries as well as its farms and fisheries. It also has boat yards which build the traditional Chinese junks, and it is the home of the Bun Festival which draws crowds from all over Hong Kong for four days each year in May. Like most other Chinese festivals, this one has a religious purpose—to give thanks and to express sorrow for all the animals, birds and fish which have been killed in the past year to provide food for people. Nevertheless, it is a happy festival, with processions, music, plays and a great deal of noise. Its main feature is the bun hills—three enormous towers of buns, each about sixty feet (eighteen meters) high. At the end of the festival, there is a tremendous scramble to get the top bun from each tower, as these are thought to bring special luck.

Peng Chau also has its industries, but these are far from modern. Here, and mainly in their own small village homes, people follow

81

the ancient Chinese handicrafts of porcelain painting, metalwork and woodcarving.

Whether they are craftsmen, fishermen or farmers, Peng Chau people are close to ancient China in other ways, too, as are the people of most outlying islands. There is little in their villages and surroundings, or in their slow-moving, unmechanized way of life, to remind a visitor that he is within a short ferry ride of bustling, westernized, jet-age, bursting-at-the-seams Central and Kowloon. Even big Lantau Island, with 30,000 people, seems part of an older world. Lantau's main features are two monasteries—one Buddhist, one Christian—and the life of the whole island seems to match the quiet ways of the monks. But Lantau Island, or at least its northern coast, may steadily lose its quiet atmosphere as Hong Kong's new airport located there becomes fully operational.

Tsing Yi is very different—but perhaps we should no longer call Tsing Yi an island. Very close to the southern shore of the New Territories, it has been joined to the mainland by a road bridge and it is now part of a new mainland city, Tsuen Wan. As a result, Tsing Yi has become much more than an island of fishermen, farmers and traditional boat-builders. It has a large chemical works, a power station which supplies much of the electricity used in the New Territories and Kowloon, a variety of modern factories and a growing spread of housing estates. Within a few years, these housing estates provided homes, mainly in tower blocks, for nearly 200,000 people.

The planners who pulled Tsing Yi into the new city of Tsuen Wan have since turned their thoughts to other islands—for example

A monk in prayer in the main temple of the Po Lin Buddhist Monastery on Lantau Island.

A view of Lantau Island.

Chek Lap Kok, which once lay off the western side of Lantau. Chek Lap Kok was a small island, just a few rocky hills too barren for farming. So the planners decided to join it to Lantau and the mainland with road bridges, and to cut the tops off the hills to make a badly-needed new airport. They have promised that this will not disturb the quiet life of Lantau very much. The road between the bridges is for airport traffic only, and the traffic is not allowed to leave it. However, Chek Lap Kok airport is the biggest of the many major engineering projects that modern Hong Kong has bravely undertaken. The airport officially opened in July of 1998 and now Lantau will judge how right the planners were.

84

8

Kowloon and The New Territories

Kowloon is the terminus of Hong Kong's railway link with China, and the main entrance to Hong Kong by sea. This means that many of the two million visitors who come to Hong Kong each year spend at least some of their time on the Kowloon side of Victoria Harbor. Indeed, the majority of them spend most of their time here, because a great deal of Hong Kong's trading with other countries is centered on Kowloon.

So it is not surprising to find that at first sight Kowloon is very much a visitor's city. Behind the ocean terminal, docks and ferry piers on the western side of the Kowloon Peninsula spreads a mass of shops and stalls and street-sellers' stands, hotels and restaurants and places of entertainment—all a startling mixture of Chinese, British and international.

With a bag full of goods from all over the world bought duty-free in the huge shopping center at the ocean terminal, a visitor may walk along Peking Road to the Sands Cinema, turn left to the Wing

On Mansion, left again down I Chang Road to Ashley Road, and there, near an Italian restaurant, he will find himself facing a doorway labelled Ned Kelly's Last Stand—The Australian Fun Pub. By way of Haiphong Road, he can then take a look at the Muslim mosque in Kowloon Park, and meet some Indians busy selling cloth in Cameron Road before he risks the teeming traffic (including very British-looking double-decker buses) of Nathan Road. Nathan Road—named after a famous Hong Kong governor of Jewish ancestry, is the busiest of all Kowloon's busy streets. And there, if our visitor is not delayed too long by attractive duty-free shops and hard-selling shopkeepers, he can have lunch at a large choice of interesting restaurants.

However, this visitors' area—called Tsim Sha Tsui—is not by any means the whole of Kowloon. North of it, as far as a high, bare yellow ridge which looks rather like a lion and is named Lion Rock, the peninsula is crammed with the homes and workplaces of about half Hong Kong's population, perhaps three times as many as live in the crowded Central District on Hong Kong Island.

This part of Kowloon, a very Chinese part, is Hong Kong's main industrial area. If you have a Hong Kong watch, a Hong Kong shirt, a Hong Kong calculator or a Hong Kong plastic bucket, the chances are very strong that it came from a Kowloon factory. Some of the factories are large and modern, with hundreds of workers and a huge output of products. Some are very small, perhaps no more than a workbench or even an old kitchen table in the cramped living room of a tiny home. And some look down on the city from skyscrapers especially built for industrial purposes. These are

The Canton Road jade market in Kowloon.

called vertical factories. They were built to provide better accommodation for some of the manufacturers who had been working in their own homes or in sheds or shanties, and they had to rise high because Hong Kong is so very short of suitable ground space.

The accommodations are certainly better, but a tower block full of small factories can be very noisy, and also dangerous. Safety precautions are not always taken very seriously in Hong Kong. A factory using materials which explode or catch fire easily might well be sharing a floor with one using naked flames, while a factory on the floor below might equally well have a stack of its products blocking the fire escape. So perhaps it is just as well that Hong Kong has a large and very efficient fire service. In a recent year the service answered 13,000 fire calls, over 6,000 calls for rescues and similar emergencies, and over 221,000 for the use of its ambulances.

Hong Kong also needs its large and very efficient police force, and not only to deal with people who try to enter as illegal immigrants. Hong Kong has been much more successful at making a living than it has been at preventing crime. Indeed, it has an unusually high number of people who make their living by crime of one kind or another. Much of this is also centered on Kowloon, where there was once a particularly crimeridden area known as The Walled City. The area is much improved now and the last of the actual walls was removed in 1976.

The walled village, Kam Tin, well outside Kowloon, near the northern edge of the New Territories, still does have walls. They

A Peking duck farm in the New Territories.

stand four-square and strong, with watch-towers at all four corners and only one gateway, and they have stood like that for nearly a thousand years. When they were built, they were needed. Attacks by invading armies or brigands, or even by pirates from the sea, were always likely. So when danger was seen from the watch-towers, the farming people of Kam Tin could come in from their fields to safety behind solid stone.

Now, Kam Tin is kept as it used to be to remind modern Hong Kong of how people lived in old China. Here in the New Territories, there are also reminders of old China outside Kam Tin–tiny, close-planted fields; sometimes a plough drawn by water buffalo; women of the Hakka tribe wearing huge, black-veiled straw hats; small groves of trees planted on the higher side of each

89

Learning Resources Center
University of Wyoming Libraries
Laramie, WY 82070

Ploughing with a water buffalo in the New Territories.

farming village, in the belief that the spirit of the wind blowing through them will keep evil away.

But the New Territories is not all old China. In some other ways, it has changed greatly since China leased it to Britain in 1898. For example, this part of the old Chinese empire used to be called The Emperor's Rice Bowl, because its soil and its climate were ideal for rice-growing. The farms could produce two crops of very good rice a year; they were still growing much of Hong Kong's rice at the end of the 1960s. But by then Hong Kong had so many people that it seemed better to bring in all their rice from other countries, and let the local farmers concentrate on growing vegetables. Now there are very few rice-fields left in the New Territories, nor anywhere else in Hong Kong. Instead, the farmers are growing vegetables in such quantities that Westerners often raise their eyebrows when they see

Flooded rice paddies. Very few now remain in Hong Kong.

how small the farms are. Many have no more than about one acre (0.4 hectare) of usable land, and yet manage to make a comfortable family living from it. Of course they have to work very hard, but they are helped by the fact that the Chinese have a long tradition of intensive farming—growing large crops in small spaces. They are also helped by the Hong Kong government, which gives them loans of money to buy equipment and fertilizers, and provides advice from experts on modern scientific farming.

For many years, the Hong Kong government left the New Territories mainly to its farmers in their six hundred small villages. With so many townspeople in Kowloon and on Hong Kong Island to be fed, it did not want factories and housing for town-workers spreading onto land which might possibly be used for growing food. But as the town population grew even bigger, it had to think again, and consider how it could build industrial and housing estates in the New Territories without any serious loss of farmland.

As a result, there are now six new cities spaced around the New Territories, most of them on the coasts. The land was found partly by reclaiming it from the sea, and partly by cutting into the sides of barren hills to make huge "shelves" on which tower blocks, factories and shopping centers could be built. In one of the new cities, Shatin, there is even room for horse-racing on a course reclaimed from the sea.

The population of the New Territories has grown to just under three million. The great majority of these are townspeople, but their farming neighbors are still producing nearly half the vegetables eaten in Hong Kong, as well as much more than half the poultry and a large number of the pigs. They are also farming fish in about 4,500 acres (1,820 hectares) of freshwater ponds.

Most of Hong Kong's pigs, and also many other foods, come in from China. These imports arrive partly by sea, and partly by the Kowloon-Canton railway, which runs right through the New Territories, and carries both goods and passengers. Passengers who wish to travel the whole distance between Kowloon and Canton may take a through express train, but all others travelling to or from China must change trains, and stations, at the border. They walk between the station on the Hong Kong side and the station on the China side, over a footbridge which has border guards at either end.

Crossing the border was once very difficult because the government of China neither encouraged visitors nor liked its own

A view of Shatin under construction—one of the new cities.

people to visit Hong Kong. Travelers needed very good reasons before they were allowed to pass either way. The crossing is still difficult but this is mainly because so many people are allowed in and out of China that the border stations are seriously overcrowded with passengers and parcels from the forty-five trains which travel the single railway line each way each day. Visitors to China are now much more welcome than they used to be, and it is also much easier for people from China to visit Hong Kong. The border is quite open to travelers who wish to go shopping in either country, and there are many Chinese who cross into Hong Kong for their daily work.

Recently, the Chinese government has agreed to help in making the border stations less crowded and more comfortable, and the

Hong Kong government has nearly finished doubling the railway line between Kowloon and the border. That will mean that trains going one way will not have to wait in sidings for trains going the other way to pass. At the same time, the trains themselves are being electrified, to make rail travel through the New Territories faster, cleaner and more comfortable.

Hong Kong is also linked to China by a water-pipeline. In the New Territories there are now two very big reservoirs made by damming inlets from the sea, and also a desalination plant for changing sea water to fresh water. However, in spite of these, even with a number of smaller reservoirs and the use of sea-water for flushing in some places, Hong Kong has only about three-fifths of the water that it needs. The rest is piped from China, and Hong Kong pays China for it.

9

Present Problems

Hong Kong and China are now under one government, and China gains greatly by having such a productive and prosperous region. Many of China's products are exported through Hong Kong. Many others are sold in China's Hong Kong shops. And Hong Kong provides work for at least a million mainland citizens.

China is also helped in her dealings with Western nations by having a free-market zone so close. For example, China has recently been developing Shenzhen–just over the border from the New Territories as a factory and tourist area. Foreign companies are being encouraged to set up factories and hotels there. This is attracting a fairly large number of foreigners, most of whom would be much less interested in Shenzhen were it not so conveniently placed just outside Hong Kong's back doorway.

As the 1980s progressed, it could not be forgotten that China was the real owner of the New Territories and had the right to reclaim it in 1997. And that this would mean Hong Kong's losing nearly all of its farmland, most of its reservoirs, most of its electricity generating stations, and a growing part of the factory industries upon which its life depended. Its inhabitants, many of them refugees from the mainland, would have crowded into Kowloon and Hong Kong Island.

Surprisingly, the British did not seem willing to undertake the responsibilities further occupation of Hong Kong would have required. A Joint Declaration was issued by Britain and China in 1984 providing for an orderly transfer of authority in 1997. A Chinese crackdown on dissidents in 1989 caused some worry in Hong Kong, but the possible loss of some voting rights belatedly introduced by the British in 1991 seemed to be outweighed by the prospects of a continuing vigorous free-market economy.

The handing over of power took place as scheduled at midnight on June 30, 1997. There were no immediate dire consequences; indeed, there were celebrations in Hong Kong and in Chinese communities around the world.

Hong Kong's population continues to grow. More babies are being born and fewer old people are dying, as social and health conditions

The wire fence is the boundary between the New Territories and China.

This notice speaks for itself—it was erected in an attempt to stop illegal immigration from China into the New Territories.

keep improving. More young people are graduating from schools and universities every year, looking for jobs or training opportunities. No one can afford to simply wait and see what the future will bring. That has never been the way of Hong Kong's people, nor the way of those who sell products there or export goods produced there. The mainland-based Bank of China has invested heavily in Hong Kong's future, as have many overseas investors.

Hong Kong's enterprising spirit has never been content with past successes, and knows that trying to stand still would mean slipping backwards, and losing much of the prosperity for which it has worked so hard. To foreign observers, it appears for the moment that Hong Kong's people are moving forward as though 1997 had never happened.

GLOSSARY

acupuncture   A medical practice involving inserting needles into pressure points of the body to ease pain and cure ailments.

boat people   Prior to 1975, a term applied primarily to Hong Kong people who spend most of their lives on boats, such as fishermen and operators of floating restaurants. Since 1975, the term has often been applied to Vietnamese refugees.

Cantonese   Chinese dialect of the province next to Hong Kong, the dominant language of the territory.

cheongsam   A traditional Chinese dress,usually worn in a more stylish modern cut in Hong Kong.

compradore   An agent for workers who sells their labor to employers for a high percentage of their salary.

Crown Colony   Hong Kong's status as part of the British Commonwealth until June 30,1997. A Royal governor ruled the territory with the assistance of an appointed group of advisors. The majority of the population were Chinese, but were treated as second-class citizens, especially before 1945.

dragon boat   A canoe-like boat, up to 100-feet long, used for

98

races during the Dragon Boat Festival in early June.

factory   In the early days of the China trade, not a place where goods were manufactured, but a warehouse and living quarters for Europeans, particularly in Canton.

ideogram   Chinese picture writing, understood by all Chinese regardless of their spoken dialect.

junk   Traditional Chinese sailing vessel, used for fishing in the Hong Kong area.

mah jong   Chinese table game played with decorative tiles.

Special Administrative Region   Hong Kong's status as part of the People's Republic of China since July 1, 1997. China exercises complete political control over the territory, but the former colony's free market system and civil liberties theoretically remain in place for at least fifty years.

Tai Chi   A traditional form of physical training, with dance-like movements similar to martial arts.

typhoon   A tropical storm of the western Pacific with heavy rain and strong winds. Typhoons generally bypass Hong Kong, but affect its weather.

Learning Resources Center
University of Wyoming Libraries
Laramie, WY 82070

INDEX